Also by Tanna Marshall
Living Peacefully in a Big City: A Guide to Maintaining Your Sanity, Health and Happiness

The Enlightened Caregiver

A Holistic Care Guide for You and Your Loved One

Tanna Marshall

BALBOA.
PRESS
A DIVISION OF HAY HOUSE

Balboa Press books may be ordered through booksellers or by contacting:

Balboa Press
A Division of Hay House
1663 Liberty Drive
Bloomington, IN 47403
www.balboapress.com
1 (877) 407-4847

Because of the dynamic nature of the Internet, any web addresses or links contained in this book may have changed since publication and may no longer be valid. The views expressed in this work are solely those of the author and do not necessarily reflect the views of the publisher, and the publisher hereby disclaims any responsibility for them.

The author of this book does not dispense medical advice or prescribe the use of any technique as a form of treatment for physical, emotional, or medical problems without the advice of a physician, either directly or indirectly. The intent of the author is only to offer information of a general nature to help you in your quest for emotional and spiritual well-being. In the event you use any of the information in this book for yourself, which is your constitutional right, the author and the publisher assume no responsibility for your actions.

Any people depicted in stock imagery provided by Thinkstock are models, and such images are being used for illustrative purposes only.
Certain stock imagery © Thinkstock.

Printed in the United States of America.

ISBN: 978-1-4525-2218-0 (sc)
ISBN: 978-1-4525-2219-7 (e)

Library of Congress Control Number: 2014917218

Balboa Press rev. date: 09/24/2014

**To my mom, Bobby
(and my Daddy in Heaven, Bob) –**
Thank you for giving me everything –
I'm just paying you back.

Contents

Acknowledgments

I want to thank:

- My Mom for giving me life, and with my Daddy always giving me everything. Little did she know that she was producing her future caregiver in the form of her "late-in-life-oops-baby.".

- My amazing support team of Anne, Cassie, David, Valerie, Laurel, Tom and Audi. I would not have any kind of a life without your assistance and giving me a break once in a while.

- My incredible husband Brad for being so unbelievably understanding, loving, supportive and helpful with my situation in caring for my mom. Not a lot of men would stick around for this kind of marriage!

- Mom's extended care team of Dr. Shin, Dr. Li, and the amazing team at One Generation, especially Valerie, Melissa, Anna, Temeka, Ophelia, Annie and Capricia.

- Brian Zick for the beautiful cover illustration and design.

- Again, my creative genius husband for imagining the concept for the cover design.

- Conni Ponturo for encouraging me and getting me excited about this project.

- Lisa De La O Wyman for lovingly proofing and editing this book.

- My coaches and colleagues who have supported and encouraged me with love on my journey – especially Maura Mark, Jamie Leff, Gina Gomez, Beth Grant and Marsh Engle.

- My friends, who are always supportive of my situation, always there for me when I need to vent, who take me when they can get me socially, and understand when I can't get away to spend time with them. I don't know what I would do without all of you. Thank you for sticking with me and helping me to have a life!

Introduction

Welcome, Enlightened Caregiver!

In this book, you will learn to take care of yourself *first*, and your loved one, in a holistic way, taking into consideration your well-being in body, mind and spirit on all levels.

Being a caregiver can be an overwhelming job, whether you are caring for an elderly relative, your spouse, a friend or neighbor, or even taking care of children. Caregiver means you are caring for someone; this covers most people on the planet. But for those of us who are in a situation where more time, energy and knowledge is required, it can be especially challenging, and often lonely and isolating. For this reason, I have written this book to provide support, information, resources and most importantly, compassion for you and your situation. I understand what you are going through.

I have been taking care of my elderly mother for many years now and I have created a routine that keeps us both healthy and happy. I am sharing many of the elements we have in place in the hope that you will find a few ideas to help you create an easier, more fulfilling and balanced experience in caring for someone else.

Just to give you a little background regarding my health practices and professional credentials – I have been studying health, healing and researching and applying natural remedies and alternative therapies for almost thirty years. I am a Certified Holistic Health Practitioner, Certified Massage Therapist, Certified Energy Worker and Certified Law of Attraction Life Coach. I was diagnosed with Lupus when I was fifteen, and after twenty-six years, I cured myself. I now help others create what they want in their lives, which often includes improved health. I have great faith in the power of nature to heal us.

There are so many elements unique to the situation of taking care of someone while you are also attempting to take care of yourself. You may think you need to put the other person first, but in this case, you have to make yourself and your own well-being your priority or you will have nothing to give. When you don't take care of yourself, you may become physically depleted, emotionally drained, angry, resentful and eventually even make yourself sick. So it may surprise you to find that the majority of this program is aimed at *you*, the caregiver, and your self-care.

Please keep in mind that this program was created from my perspective and my personal experience not only as a daughter and caregiver, but also a Certified Holistic Health Practitioner and a Certified Life Coach specializing in the Law of Attraction. You may not understand or agree with everything I am sharing here and that is okay. Just know that it comes from my heart and from my experience of what has worked for me and many others. Take what resonates with you and leave the rest. My intention and desire is that you will find some valuable information here that you can apply to your specific situation.

Preface

How Did I Get Here?

I wanted to share my story about how I came to be a full-time caregiver for my mother because we all arrive at this place in different ways…

My father was in and out of the hospital for about two years beginning on Christmas Day, 2001. We thought we were going to lose him several times, so the fact that he stuck around for another two years amazed me. Sometimes I couldn't believe he was still here. I often felt that he had outsmarted death and spent more time here with us than he was supposed to, and I appreciated every moment of that "extra" time.

When his health began to decline at a faster rate, we knew that his time was almost up - and we were all accepting of that since we had had so much time to prepare for those final days.

This next part of the story really demonstrates how the Universe is always working on our behalf and making things work out in ways we never could have imagined on our own. It's important to understand that I live my life by the Law of Attraction because it is very real, and I have created my life by utilizing these principles since I first learned about them many years ago. They have worked so well for me that I have become a Certified Law of Attraction Life Coach.

So that I don't alienate anyone, know that when I use the term Universe, it is the same as God, Higher Power, The Divine, Source Energy – they're all just different labels for the same Omnipresent Energy that is available to all of us all the time. And if you really look at it, the Law of Attraction is basically the same as what Jesus was teaching:

> "And in all things, whatsoever ye shall ask believing, ye shall receive them." (Mark 11:24)

> "If thou canst believe, all things are possible to him that believeth." (Mark 9:23)

> "According to your faith be it done unto you." (Matthew 9:29)

You don't have to be a Christian or even religious to appreciate these powerful messages from a great spiritual teacher.

Are we all on the same page now? Okay, good! If these ideas seem foreign or weird to you, just stick with me and hopefully you will relax into it. You may even get excited about the power that lies within you to not only consciously create your own life experience, but positively influence the lives of those around you. It could especially color your role as caregiver and positively benefit your loved one in wonderful new ways.

About a month before my father's health drastically declined, I sprained my foot and had to stay with my parents for a few weeks because it was too hard to get up and down the stairs to my apartment on crutches. During this time, I was also looking for a new place to live – I wanted some kind of single-story house with a yard, with walls free of neighbors directly on the other side.

This special situation allowed me to be there when my father wound up in the emergency room and they informed him that unless he underwent dialysis, his days were numbered. He had been saying, "I'm ready to go!" for years, usually to my tearful response of "I'm not ready for you to go!" He would then recant his declaration and assure me that he was not going anywhere for a while. But this time, we all knew it was his time. I even said to him, "Well, you've been saying you're ready to go for a while, so here is your ticket."

We brought him home and began the process of making his final days as pleasant and comfortable as possible. We got a hospital bed for him (that went into my old room), and obtained hospice care to assist and relieve my mom once in a while. I was still hobbling to work every day, saying goodbye to him in the morning and spending the evenings sitting by his bed talking or just watching TV at his side. One of my favorite moments was during an episode of *All in the Family* – my father loved that show and in many ways was very much like Archie Bunker. It was the episode with Sammy Davis Jr.; if you're familiar with the show you know the one I'm talking about. Archie is about to take a picture with Sammy and at the last minute, just as the picture is being taken, Sammy kisses Archie on the cheek. My father wasn't even watching the TV – he was lying down with his eyes closed just listening. But I heard a long, hearty chuckle from him at that moment during the show.

We had a lot of great talks – I told him how wonderful it would be when his spirit finally let go of this body that was pained and no longer serving him. I made him promise to make his presence known and to be at my wedding one day. I also asked him to please communicate with me when he was gone so I would know it was him, and on several occasions I also told him that it was okay to go. In his dry humor he would reply, "Go where?"

It was also during these conversations that he requested that I move in with my mother and help take care of her after he died. At the time she did not require much care, being very self-sufficient, in spite of the fact that she had lost the sight in her left eye the previous year. She had a freak accident at a gardening store where she tripped on some floor mats and with nowhere to brace herself, fell into a row of gardening gloves, impaling her eye on one of the hooks. I know – gross. It was awful, but it was also a bit of a miracle because even though that hook severed her optic nerve, it also came within one eighth of an inch from puncturing her brain and killing her. Her doctor told her she should go buy a lottery ticket. I was caregiver to both her and my father for a while after that incident. Thank goodness I had such an understanding boss at the time for all the work I missed.

I think my father was planning ahead to where we are now, knowing that mom would eventually need more care, and wanting her to have company in the house after he was gone. I am very grateful that I had a chance to ease into this role over a few years instead of having it all fall on me in its current form. I would have been totally overwhelmed, so I understand that feeling if you now find yourself in this role unexpectedly.

We had an interesting interval during those last seven weeks of my father's life. Due to all the time I had spent helping with my father, spending every weekday lunch hour driving to the hospital to be with him and then the subsequent time missed from work after my mother's accident, my parents sent me to Hawaii to relax. We had planned this trip before my father's last incident and it put me in a difficult position. The trip to Hawaii was to see a good friend that I had made during my years at Capitol Records, Martin Denny. Martin, who is a legend in Exotica music, had invited me to come visit him on numerous occasions, so I finally planned the trip. Martin was ninety-three years old at this point and I was so torn: should I cancel my trip while my father is dying or go see Martin while he is still around and we have a date that works for us both?

My father was adamant about me going, so I did, with the request that he not go anywhere while I was gone. I called twice a day demanding to speak directly to him to make sure he was still there, and apparently he told people who visited him that he was indeed waiting for me to return.

I had a wonderful trip and visit with Martin, and was happy to find my father still there when I got back. In fact, he stopped eating a few weeks after that and somehow hung on another three weeks! I resumed my daily visits with him every evening, not always talking as much as just being with him.

We had to give him morphine to keep him comfortable and eventually increase the dosage daily, so basically he was unconscious for most of his last week here.

One day when I was getting ready to go to work, there was a hummingbird outside my bathroom window, hovering close like it was saying "Good morning!" I had never seen one there before and it was a wonderful start to my day. I went to kiss my father goodbye and headed off to work. A half-hour after I began my work day, my mother called and told me that he was gone. I believe that his spirit was in that hummingbird, already having departed even though his physical body was still breathing. Hummingbirds continue to hover in front of and around me all the time, and I know that it's my Daddy saying hello and honoring his promise to stay close and communicate with me.

I will always be grateful for this amazing quality time that I had with my father the last seven weeks of his life, and I am honored to be able to make the last years of my mother's life as healthy, happy and enjoyable as possible. Although every once in a while I think, "Thanks a lot, Daddy – what did you get me into??" I always feel his response, "I know, Little Girl... it can be hard, but you are doing a great job and I am proud of you! Hang in there..."

I now want to help *you* hang in there while you do your best to create the most happy, healthy and pleasant experience for your loved one, while attempting to maintain your own sanity and well-being.

So let's begin with YOU!

YOU FIRST –
The Fine Art of Self Care

I want to make it abundantly clear that YOU must be your first priority. Often caregivers (and women in general) feel guilty about taking care of themselves and putting their own needs above those around them.

Remember the safety speech you hear on the airplane every time you board a flight, about putting on YOUR oxygen mask first and then assisting your child with theirs? Same principle – if you don't take care of yourself first, you won't have anything to give to anyone else; or, in the extreme example used on the airplane, you might be dead. What good are you to anybody then?

We were not meant to run ourselves into the ground and sacrifice our own well-being for that of everyone else around us. If this is how you have been operating, the people around you probably expect you to give 100% all the time and don't give it a second thought. They think you're fine and that you love it. Be prepared for a little push-back when you finally begin setting boundaries to put yourself first, and perhaps even ask them to pitch in and help.

I know there may be deep-rooted issues behind allowing yourself not only to care for yourself but also to (gasp!) pamper yourself and luxuriate once in a while... perhaps even totally disconnect and have some fun! All I can say is it's time to get over that and learn to love yourself. You are deserving and worthy of the best of everything. The better cared for you are and the better you feel, the better care you will be able to provide for your loved ones.

Repeat after me: "I am deserving and worthy of love, care, luxury and fun! I am just as important as anyone else and I now know that it is in everyone's best interest that I make my wants, needs and desires my first priority."

You are never neglecting anyone when you love yourself enough to take good care of yourself. Okay, are we clear on that now? Good – let's move on.

Get Support

As soon as you step into the role of Caregiver, make sure you enlist family, friends, neighbors, or even paid help to give you a break once in a while so you can live your own life. Check your loved one's health insurance to find out if support or assistance is covered. It is vital that you do not feel alone or you will easily get overwhelmed, run-down, resentful, angry and possibly sick. That that is not good for you or the person you are caring for.

Please be confident in speaking up and saying, "I need help." You may be surprised who will come to your aid. But please ask. If everyone thinks you have it all together, they may not even think to offer to help. You deserve regular breaks and it is vital for you to have them so that you can continue giving your best to your loved one.

Remember that you are not alone. The number of caregivers has been steadily increasing over the years and it is taking a toll on many lives. In the past few years alone, the concerns and real-life impact of caregivers has become much more prominent. According to statistics from an article dated April 26th 2011 from www.Caring.com, "Depression Levels Among Caregivers More Than Two Times National Average, Caring.com's Newest Study Reveals", over 80% of caregivers state that their situation impacts their work situation and that they also suffer from depression. Over a third of the caregivers studied spent more than thirty hours a week on tasks caring for a loved one and over 70% were concerned about their own finances. Many caregivers are also dealing with insomnia due to their situation while facing their own health issues, which just adds to the stress of having to focus on caring for someone else and often neglecting their own well-being.

I'm sure you might be able to relate to many of these statistics in your own situation. Knowing about the growing numbers of caregivers and the potential consequences of being in this situation is why I wrote this book. While I can relate to some of the facts stated above, I am very grateful that I have been able to keep my mental, emotional, physical and spiritual health in a very good place over the years (for the most part), due to my ever-changing and diligent self-care practice. I want to help you create your own routines so that you may continue to thrive in all areas of your life while you are caring for someone else. Let me reassure you, it *is* possible. You just need to find what works for you and have the appropriate support in place.

There are a plethora of resources available to help you create your own self-care practice and to support you in your role as a caregiver, but the search can be overwhelming and you may not have the energy to pursue it. I encourage you to do your own search online for the help that feels good to you, but here are a few resources to get you started with information, support, education, tools and facts that may be useful to you:

www.caring.com/caregiving-research
www.caregiver.com
www.caregiver.org
www.aarp.org/home-family/caregiving/
www.medicare.gov/campaigns/caregiver/caregiver-resource-kit.html

You may feel totally alone much of the time, and I want you to know that you have more support available to you than you realize. I am here for you right now in the form of this book and there are plenty of others out there who want to support you as well. Just reach out and ask. I know it can be hard but you need it and you deserve it. I assure you, people will be happy and eager to help if you just ask. You are loved and all is well.

Now let's focus on some ways you can cultivate your well-being and nurture yourself.

Find a Support Group
that Empowers You

You may find it helpful to join a support group with members who are in the same situation that you are. Not everyone understands what we go through as full-time caregivers and how mentally, emotionally and physically draining it can be. There are many groups available to you, so do some research and see if there is one that feels good to you. If you are unable to physically attend a group or can't find one in your area, many are now offering group support calls or online chat forums for caregivers. Here are several resources to get you started:

www.caregiver.com
www.leezascareconnection.org

I have attended several support groups over the years and enjoyed connecting with other caregivers. I discovered that I needed to be selective about the groups I attended because often they were only opportunities for people to commiserate about their situation. I understand the need to vent your frustrations. It's necessary so that your feelings can be expressed without building up inside of you like a pressure cooker. Sometimes you just need someone to listen. However, I don't enjoy an atmosphere of continual negative complaining without much positive input. That just brings everybody down. Personally, I need to have uplifting support, even if there is no easy resolution to my issue. It's important as a caregiver to have compassion for yourself and also around you in a supportive environment. It's easy to get caught up in the drama of others' situations, but that negative spiral and buildup of momentum ultimately will not serve anyone. You want to find a group that makes you feel loved and supported while you are there and uplifted and encouraged when you leave. I'm not comfortable in a perpetually negative environment, so I learned which groups were good for me and which to leave behind. Please do the same and only attend groups that feel good to you. It's important to protect your energy, which is so easily influenced when you are tired, worn out or feeling vulnerable, so always surround yourself with the most positive people and situations.

It can be difficult for me to be in situations that may not be serving the purpose they are intended to, especially as a Law of Attraction Life Coach. I have a deep understanding and appreciation of the fact that we all create our own reality with our thoughts and beliefs, regardless of our current circumstances. From that perspective, I found it frustrating to listen to people who were feeling stuck and perpetually creating what they did not want, and yet even *more* of what they did not want, by continually complaining about it. I have great compassion for these people so it made my heart hurt to listen to them staying stuck emotionally, when I knew that they could improve their situation if they had the tools, information and support to make positive changes. We always have the power to change our emotional vibration, and therefore our experience, even if only in our mind.

These groups were obviously not an appropriate forum for me to share my beliefs and help these people to get their thoughts going in a better direction. All I could do was hold my higher vibration with the intention of uplifting their energy, even if they didn't consciously realize it.

I also came across some people who were very committed to their role of "helpless victim", continually focusing on all the bad things that kept happening and worrying about what would go wrong next. This can become a habitual thought resulting in an ongoing experience and the only relief may seem to come from talking about it, especially if you are in a group that enjoys commiserating with each other. Unfortunately, that only creates more of the same. But this book *is* the appropriate forum for me to reach like-minded people like you who want to take back your power in the creation of your life, even as a caregiver. I want you to understand that you always have a choice about how you view your situation, and therefore can create an experience that feels better to you. You are never a victim and you are more powerful than you realize.

It is very empowering to know that you can drastically shift your experience by consciously choosing your thoughts and being aware of your emotions. I know that since you are reading this book, you have made the choice to consciously create some changes to improve your experience. Good for you! I am here to support you in that 100%. In fact, I have created a feminine support community called *Infinite Woman* just for women to receive consistent help, guidance and support on a regular basis. If you'd like to join us or just have more information, please visit www.infinitewoman.com/Membership.html

Please know that you don't have to do this alone. There are communities out there who understand what you are going through, and an abundance of resources available for support. Check out your options and find the one that is right for you.

Get Paid for Your Services through Government Programs

If you have had to give up your job to care for someone or if your loved one has limited resources, there are specific government programs that might pay you for your caregiving services:

www.medicare.gov/campaigns/caregiver/caregiver.html
www.usa.gov/Citizen/Topics/Health/caregivers.shtml

Depending on your situation, you may be eligible to get paid for your services. I learned about this from a friend who has a daughter with a disability, and his wife was able to receive payment from the government for caring for their child. This is definitely a job and deserves to be compensated, if possible.

I don't have much experiential knowledge about this since our situation doesn't quality for payment for me as full-time caregiver, but I want to make sure that you have the resources to find out for yourself. Fortunately, we are comfortable financially and I am grateful that we always have the funds we need. Not everyone is as fortunate, so please look into these resources and see what is available for you.

Have a Creative Outlet for Fun

I find that a great source of depression and anxiety is when we are not expressing ourselves creatively. It doesn't matter what we enjoy, be it music, art, sports, reading, puzzles, knitting, movies – we need something that is just for our enjoyment, where we feel we are expressing ourselves in a way that brings us joy. When we don't have that creative flow and enjoyment in our lives, part of us dies.

Find something you enjoy doing just for the sake of doing it. Something that takes you out of your reality for a little while, that helps you lose track of time when you are involved and engrossed in it. This doesn't mean that you necessarily have to be creating something, just involved in something that you enjoy.

You don't have to get overly involved in a new hobby or an overwhelming project. This can be as simple as taking the time to read a magazine or a novel just for entertainment. No need to put pressure on yourself to be creative if you feel you're not a creative person. This is meant to relieve some of your stress, not to cause more! Just stay on the lookout for things you think you might enjoy doing and try them out whenever something new looks interesting to you.

Perhaps you have always wanted to try painting or writing or learning to play an instrument. It's never too late to do something new. This could be the thing that breathes life back into you – something you discover you love that is just for you. When you find that thing that nurtures your spirit, do it as often as possible.

It is imperative that you find ways to express yourself and feed your soul. Wayne Dyer has a saying that I love: "Don't die with your music still inside you." Whatever your "music" is, there is something in your heart and soul that wants to be expressed in the world, so find a way to let it out and most importantly, enjoy it!

Keep a Journal

There are probably a million things going through your mind all the time and it's good to get them out of your head and write them down regularly. Most likely you are going through a wide range of emotions every day so documenting how you feel can be cathartic. Sometimes when we feel very alone and that no one understands what we are going through, we can turn to our journal and confide how we really feel, things that we normally wouldn't share with anyone else. This is a great place for you to express whatever is on your mind freely. No one will ever see it unless you decide to share, so let it all out! It's a great release for your emotions and an opportunity to feel support, if only from a blank book that unconditionally allows you to vent the possibly unspeakable things you may be thinking or feeling. It's okay; there's no judgment from your loyal journal.

It's also a nice way to record the experience of being with your loved one that you will most likely look back at and treasure. It can also help you in the future to refer back to a previous situation and how you may have chosen to handle it differently. Additionally, you can also chart your growth and emotional development during this experience.

A journal is a great place to write down your concerns, vent your anger and explore your goals and dreams while you are in this situation. Yes, you can have goals and dreams while you are focusing on the care of someone else – in fact, it is imperative. We will discuss this in the next chapter.

Plan for Your Future

Do you take any time to think about what you want for yourself? Where do you see yourself and how do you want to be living your life five or ten years from now?

It's easy to put your future plans on the backburner because you don't ever really know when that future will be attainable. But I assure you, it is incredibly important to plan something that feels good and gets you excited about your future, even if it just feels like a fantasy right now. You never know what will come of it. Whatever you focus your attention on now will manifest in some form later. I refer often to the importance of always having something to look forward to because it keeps you enthusiastic about life. It is equally, if not more, important in this instance.

Even if you feel you can't make any concrete plans for what you will do when your loved one is gone, and perhaps you feel guilty about even entertaining the thought, it is crucial for your sanity to look beyond where you are now and think of or dream about where you'd like to be. Let your imagination run wild – what does your ideal life look like? What would you like to be doing? Where would you like to live? Dream big! Write down your dreams, goals and desires. Have a creative outlet for those dreams. If you are able to take some actual, physical steps toward the life of your dreams now, then do it! For example, I would love to move to Palm Springs later when I have the freedom to do so. So right now my husband and I go for the weekend whenever possible and I enjoy and savor every minute we have there. I fully appreciate all of the friends we have made in shops and restaurants who treat us like old friends. I even signed up for the mailing list of a local realtor and I receive emails with homes listed for sale so I can shop for my dream home. Even though this dream is a ways off in the future, these things get me into the feeling of it and make me incredibly happy and excited. Find something that does the same for you and your future plans.

The role of caregiver can be so all-consuming that if you do not have something that gives you an identity and something to look forward to outside of this situation, you may find yourself completely lost, not knowing who you are or what your purpose in life is after your loved one is gone. Discover who you are. Go within. Ask for guidance. Dream, imagine, and play in your mind. Let go, and have fun with it. Decide what you want. You don't have to do anything now, just enjoy the dream. But most importantly, *have* a dream. Just like the song "Happy Talk" says, "You've got to have a dream… if you don't have a dream… how you gonna make that dream come true?"

You deserve to have your dream *now* if for no other reason than that it makes you feel good and gives you hope for your future beyond your current situation.

Maintain Your Own Life
as Much as Possible

I know it can be difficult to get away and maintain your social life and activities while caring for your loved one (especially if you are the primary and/or live-in caregiver), but it is crucial that you get out of the house and stay connected to the outside world as often as possible. This is one area where you definitely want to have support and reinforcements in place to relieve you of your duties once in a while.

Let's explore some options:

* Get Out and See People

Make sure that your friends, co-workers, colleagues, clients and any other people in your life understand your situation and are patient with you as you make plans that work around your responsibilities. We can't always leave our loved one alone for long, if at all. But if you can get away for lunch or dinner a few times a month to reconnect with friends, it will go a long way to renewing your spirit and giving you a well-deserved break. You need some interaction with people outside of your life of caregiving to remind you that there is a big, wonderful world still out there and available to you!

* Go Out and Play (aka, Plan Fun Activities That You Enjoy)

This is my specialty! I love to have fun, and I believe it is crucial for our well-being. This can be anything that helps you relax, connect with your spirit and replenish your energy. Often, as adults, we don't make time for fun, or we view it as being irresponsible. Fun is just for kids... right? Wrong!!

Sometimes we even forget *how* to have fun – or we don't know what *is* fun for us anymore. If this is you, then I'm going to suggest that you spend some time considering what you really enjoy doing and whose company you enjoy. When you combine these two elements, you have the recipe for a fulfilling feast for your soul. Perhaps you can develop a routine where you and a friend do something fun on a regular basis. When you have something to look forward to, it makes your daily routine more tolerable, because you know you have some fun coming up.

I consider this step mandatory, and I plan my schedule accordingly. I make sure that I have regular "girl time" with my ladies (my girlfriends are a major priority in my life); time to be outside in nature either in my hammock or my little pool; time to read or watch a movie just for the enjoyment of it (I am a bit addicted to health research and personal development material, but I sneak in the occasional novel), and last and most importantly, a minimum of one Disneyland day a month. It may sound odd to you but this has become a crucial part of my wellness routine. I have an annual pass and am fortunate to have several friends who are also annual pass holders with flexible schedules who enjoy a day of fun and magic as much as I do. I believe it's comparable to men who love to go golfing as often as they can to escape their regular routine out on the golf course. We all need some form of that "getting away from it all". What's yours? Having fun will keep you young and vibrant in spirit.

One of my favorite episodes of *The Twilight Zone* addresses this very issue – "Kick the Can". I suggest you watch it; you will better understand the magic of getting out to play, having fun, and how it keeps you young, happy, healthy and sane.

*   Relax and Minimize Stress

You're probably thinking, "I don't have time to relax!" Well here's the thing: if you don't find a way to include relaxation in your daily routine, you are potentially inviting a whole slew of physical, mental and emotional problems. The root of just about every illness we face is because our bodies have been in a state of chronic stress for way too long. Most of us were not taught how to relax and in fact, it's been beat into us that relaxing is the equivalent of being lazy. Our culture has created generations of workaholics who are running themselves into the ground without much information about how to relax and play to maintain good health. This habit of stress is usually developed way before any physical problems occur so it is to your benefit to practice preventative relaxation. Fortunately, this topic is coming more to the forefront these days, even supported by major corporations who understand and appreciate the fact that happy and relaxed employees are healthy and productive employees.

There has been even more attention brought to this topic by Dr. Lissa Rankin, author of *Mind Over Medicine: Scientific Proof That You Can Heal Yourself.* I highly recommend you read this book to help overcome any physical problems you may be having or as a preventative tool if you are already in good health. Dr. Rankin thoroughly explores the consequences of chronic stress in our lives and teaches you how to make your own diagnosis of your health and then how to create a prescription designed to heal your life on all levels. I was thrilled to find a medical doctor who understands and promotes the principles that I have believed in, lived by and taught to my clients for years!

So let's get back to the potential issue of when and how to relax. You can always find ways to fit in a few moments to close your eyes and breathe. In between tasks around the house or while out running errands, at a stoplight in the car, in the checkout line while shopping or at the bank, in the shower, in the kitchen cooking or washing dishes…you get the idea. If your schedule is that jam-packed, try these suggestions to get started.

Relaxing is different for everyone and what might be relaxing to me might not resonate with you. I love to make time to be quiet and read a book or magazine. I love to get outside and spend time in my hammock or go for a walk. Sometimes I just sit and listen to the birds and watch the wind blowing in the trees and the clouds floating by. If you can just stop what you're doing and find a way to get quiet and to connect with your inner source of peace even just for a moment, you will feel the benefit and I'm sure you will make a point of working it into your daily schedule, regardless of how busy you are.

Meditation is one of the best ways you can begin a relaxation practice, even if you just start with a minute a day and work up to ten minutes a day. All you have to do is find a comfortable place to sit or lie down where you will not be disturbed for a few minutes (I do most of my relaxation practices while Mom is asleep in the morning, during her afternoon nap or after she goes to bed at night), close your eyes, focus on your breath and empty your mind of all thought. This can be difficult due to our constantly busy monkey-mind, but when thoughts come up, just let them go and focus back on your breathing. I like to put my attention in between my heart and solar plexus and envision a bright light emanating out to the rest of my body, illuminating all of my chakras (energy centers), sending out good vibes that surround me with only good things that match this wonderful vibration. Did I just get a little too "woo woo" for some of you? That's okay – just try it and see how you feel. Isn't trying something new and weird worth the benefit of it helping you relax?

Try whatever resonates with you now that you have some ideas of how you can fit relaxation into your days.

   * Spend Plenty of Quality Time with Your
     Significant Other

If you have a significant other, your caregiving situation can be a strain on your primary relationship. This not exclusively a romantic partner; this can be anyone who is close to you and is a regular source of love, support and encouragement. It can be a best friend, a neighbor, a coworker or a relative you are close to.

Hopefully you have someone who understands and supports you in your responsibilities, is there to listen to you and helps you out whenever possible.

I am fortunate to be married to the most understanding, loving and supportive man on the planet. We have a very unconventional situation because my husband and I actually do not live together. I was already taking care of my mother when he came back into my life (we had broken up for three years before we got married), so we just resumed from where I was in my situation taking care of Mom and it happened to work out fine for both of us. It works to my advantage so I can be here full-time for Mom, but I've also discovered that I like having my own space and so does he. Our situation requires that we carefully plan our time together or we could easily go without seeing each other for weeks if things become too busy or if I don't have enough coverage for Mom while I'm away. We greatly appreciate our quality time together, and we have a wonderful marriage because of it.

I know that this is not the norm and that you are most likely in a more conventional living situation, trying to juggle everyone and everything with your caregiving responsibilities. Either way, it takes forethought and a real commitment to make quality time in your schedule for you and your significant other. You may feel torn because you often have to neglect your partner to take care of your loved one. Just remember that you are only one person, there is only so much of you to go around and you only have so much to give. Everyone has to be understanding and patient, knowing that you are doing your best and giving what you can. I hope that you have someone who goes the extra mile to give to help you out with the enormous task you have taken on. My husband is amazing and never complains, no matter how much of our quality time (or "Golden Time", as he likes to call it) is cut into by my ever-growing, time-consuming responsibilities with my mom. I am so blessed and I am incredibly grateful for this amazing man every day. I don't know what I would do without him.

Now if you are flying solo, there are pros and cons. Pro: one less person to try to please, take care of and make time for. Con: one less person to support you in this situation. But not to worry – I believe the right person is out there for everyone, and I am holding the intention that (if you so desire) your perfect person is on their way to you and will add much love, light, laughter and support to your life. This is a whole other subject that I will not get into here, but just trust that whatever your situation is at this time, it is exactly the way it is supposed to be and it is all working out for your highest good. If there is no partner in your life right now, lean a little more on your closest friends – they will understand. You need as much support as you can get. You deserve it and your real friends will be there for you – and so will that perfect person eventually.

*   Pamper Yourself

I know that it's not always in the budget to get a massage, get your hair done, or get a manicure or pedicure; but if it is, do it! You need to feel pampered and taken care of once in a while to recharge your batteries. You can't keep giving and giving without burning out. Making your personal care a priority (with a touch of luxury added) will go a long way in keeping you going as a caregiver. No doubt you are performing some of these services for your loved one from time to time – cutting and filing nails, back and foot rubs, etc. You deserve the same treatment.

There are ways to make this work if you are on a limited budget. Check out local schools for discounted services. Beauty schools provide haircuts, color and nail services, and massage schools provide massages at a fraction of the cost of going to a salon or spa. The best thing about the massage students is that they are still learning so they will take their time and you will receive an amazing, slow, relaxing massage. I know – I was that student once.

There are also a lot of little places popping up offering twenty-minute foot massages for very low prices. Sometimes that can be just enough to get you through the week.

If you are in the Los Angeles area, there is a fabulous resource called Beauty Bus Foundation, which is a non-profit organization that delivers dignity, hope and respite to terminally or chronically ill men, women, children and their caregivers through beauty and grooming services and pampering products. Programs focus on clients with ALS (Lou Gehrig's Disease), multiple sclerosis, muscular dystrophy, Parkinson's disease, spinal cord injury, cancer, stroke, other select neuromuscular and motor neuron diseases - and their caregivers. You can learn more about them here – www.beautybus.org.

You can always just get outside – go for a walk, visit a park or the beach or spend time with a friend. If you are able to, my favorite recommendation is to get a hammock! I feel this is one of the best investments you can make for your well-being. Even if you don't have an outdoor space, there are portable versions or you can install hooks in any room and enjoy. There is nothing like it for relaxing.

It is crucial that you have a break from your responsibilities on a regular basis, especially for personal care. When you look good and are relaxed, you feel better and have more to give to your loved one. You need time to leave all of your daily responsibilities behind and just enjoy yourself once in a while.

* Move Your Body

It may not be so easy to incorporate an exercise routine into your current situation. You may not have the time, the energy, the finances or the ability to get out to a class or the gym. I completely understand. I have always preferred to exercise at home and for some of the reasons stated above, I usually work out to a DVD or do my own workout routine three or four days a week. I vary my workout depending on how I am feeling and what's going on in my body. I love to walk and do some strength training with weights, abdomen crunches, yoga, Pilates and stretching. I look forward to my routine because I can do it easily at home, it doesn't take much time and I find it relaxing and enjoyable.

If you feel overwhelmed by the idea of trying to fit an effective workout routine into your daily schedule, you might enjoy looking into interval training, which only takes about 20 minutes. This routine consists of a warm up, followed by quick intervals of high intensity exercise for 30 seconds, a recovery period of 90 seconds then repeating the burst of high-intensity intervals with the recovery periods for up to 20 minutes, or whatever time frame works best for you. You can adjust the movements and intensity to your personal preference or stamina level. This is a great alternative workout that you can do at home, without exercise equipment, for free. There are plenty of online videos and tutorials to walk you through a sample routine so I encourage you to check it out.

If you spend much of your day sitting at a desk and not having that much physical activity, it helps to break up that sedentary routine just to stand up and stretch or walk in place every 15-30 minutes. Also, try to get outside several times during your day to breathe some fresh air and get away from your computer. You will come back refreshed and more productive.

If you are able to get out and take a walk, that is wonderful for getting your body moving, and also for getting outside for a little fresh air. It's easy, it's free and it's good for your whole being. If you have a beautiful place to walk where you can enjoy nature and allow it to nurture your spirit and clear your mind then you've just had a fabulous holistic workout. Whatever you choose, do it regularly and move that body! Find something that you enjoy that will fit into your schedule. It's important for your health and well-being that you enjoy and perhaps even look forward to an exercise routine that gets your body moving.

* Mind Your Mood

Keep in mind that your loved one will always reflect your emotional state back to you, just as children do to their parents. When you are feeling tired, impatient or frustrated, do you notice that those around you make you feel even more so? Others pick up on your emotions even if they don't realize it, and it can affect their emotional state, especially someone who may not be totally "there" mentally anymore and therefore unconscious of their reactions.

I know that when I'm feeling tired or impatient, my mom will seem to be intentionally doing things to annoy and frustrate me, which just exacerbates how I am feeling, and I become even more impatient with her. Then we both feel awful. But when I am feeling good, Mom is always more alert, relaxed and responsive. It's really amazing to observe.

If things are irritating or upsetting you more than usual, take a moment to get quiet and ask yourself what you need. Do you need a few minutes alone, away from your loved one? Do you need to get away and spend some time with friends? Do you need to relax with a warm bath or a good book? Do you need to escape into a movie? Figure out how you can nurture yourself and do it as soon as possible. You will notice that the better, happier and more balanced you feel, the more receptive your loved one will be to your guidance and care.

* Have a Source of Spiritual Support

Now that we have talked about taking care of you on the outside, let's talk about the inside. It's very important that we all have a source that we go to for spiritual guidance and inner strength. This is a highly personal issue for everyone, so whatever works for you is perfect. Whatever you want to call it – God, Source, Higher Self, Inner Knowing, The Divine, Infinite Intelligence, Spirit, Universe – it's all the same. Just know that it is always there to support you whenever you ask for help or guidance.

Perhaps you go to church or temple and have a built-in support community. That's a great resource to help you out and keep you going. Make sure you communicate your situation with that community; I'm sure there will be offers of assistance coming from the good people there.

If you prefer to do your own thing privately, there are plenty of resources available to you as well. You have your choice of books, CDs, television programs, online communities – all ready to provide the spiritual support and nurturing that you need.

One of my favorite resources that I turn to regularly is *Guideposts*, founded by Norman Vincent Peale. The author of the ever-popular *The Power of Positive Thinking* founded an extensive community that is still thriving today. Check out the abundance of information and support available on their website www.guideposts.com.

I have also been following Louise Hay for almost thirty years, beginning with her ground-breaking book, *You Can Heal Your Life,* which I read for the first time when I was twenty-one and still read on a regular basis and refer to often. Louise has founded the largest spiritual publishing company on the planet, also with a very large selection of books, CDs, online and live events, an online radio station and other inspirational products. You can find it all at www.hayhouse.com.

I discovered the minister Joel Osteen on TV when my father was dying. My first thought was, "Oh God, not another televangelist…" Well, he turned out to be exactly that – not another televangelist. Joel's eternally optimistic messages about hope, faith and God's unwavering love and support are always uplifting and inspiring. I never go a week without watching Joel's televised messages. Although it is a Christian program, I believe anyone would enjoy the messages. They are always exactly what I need to hear at the perfect time. It could be so for you too. Check your local listings for viewing times, or on his website, www.joelosteen.com.

Non-denominational churches are becoming more prominent these days and can be a good alternative for anyone who is not comfortable with organized religion. The Church of Religious Science (or Science of Mind), Unity, New Thought, Baha'i and Agape are all churches that are based on love, power of the mind and a belief in an Omnipresent energy/life force/Divine Power. There is only love, acceptance and support for you in these communities.

Whatever you decide, please choose something. It is imperative to know that you are not alone on this journey of your life, especially as a caregiver.

Allow Yourself the
Occasional Meltdown

Once in a while, everything that you have taken on may feel overwhelming, and you may feel hopeless and helpless. That's okay. Allow yourself a tantrum either on your own, or vent to someone you trust. Pound on some pillows, scream into a pillow or in your car, or have a good cry. You need that release often, otherwise it will build up inside of you and could manifest in unwanted ways like illness or injury, so let it out!

My husband is great at just listening to me vent my frustrations and concerns whether I need advice or not. Really, at these times, you just need someone to be present and listen. We need to feel seen and heard since most of the time our attention is focused on making sure our loved one is feeling loved, secure, happy and healthy. We need the same attention, and often all we really require is someone to be there for us.

At other times, we might want to be alone and curl up into a ball and lie in bed. That's okay too.

Since most caregivers are women, we are also dealing with monthly hormonal changes which can exacerbate a situation where we are already feeling overwhelmed. This provides even more reason to make sure you are finding balance within yourself so that your meltdowns don't turn nuclear. Be kind to yourself and give yourself whatever you need to feel better. Have some chocolate. Pet your cat. Hug a stuffed animal. Have that support system in place and on stand-by for those times when you need someone to lean on. Allow yourself to be vulnerable. We can easily get caught up in perfectionism, and not ever wanting to appear weak or that we don't totally have it together. No one expects you to be perfect or operate like a machine. You are a human being, doing the best you can, and sometimes your system goes into overload. Step back, take the pressure off and give yourself a break. You deserve that meltdown. Let it happen and don't worry about what others think. Anyone who is in the same situation as you will totally understand – and quite honestly, no one else matters anyway. You will feel better afterward, I promise.

Appreciate Where You Are

It may not have been your life's ambition to become a caretaker. Some days you may wonder, "How did I get here?" But remember that this is a special gift that you have been given – to fill someone's life with love and make it the best it can be, often during their final years on earth. Remember good times with your loved one, what they have added to your life, and what a blessing it is to honor them with the amazing gift of your care now. My parents were always extremely generous and did everything for me, so I feel it is the least I can do to honor my father's last request and repay my mother by taking care of her now.

One day, believe it or not, you will look back at this time as one of the most precious, special times of your life. Granted, you may be looking back while exhausted and feeling some sense of relief, and that is okay. It is an all-consuming job and can be very emotionally confusing. Just appreciate the wonderful moments and try to leave the rest, knowing you will one day have an extra angel watching over you.

Acknowledge and Appreciate Yourself

This is a massive responsibility that you have taken on, so make sure to step back and remember what an amazing contribution you are making not only to this person's life, but to the world, just by doing what you are doing. The love and care you are providing are sending love and light out to everyone around you.

There will be people in your life who acknowledge what you do and comment on how much they admire and respect you for it. Others have no real concept of the gravity of your situation and think that maybe you're not doing things exactly as they should be done. There may be friends of your loved one who don't fully grasp the full extent of what you deal with every day. They may criticize and offer their opinions from their perspective, which can often be upsetting, but take it with a grain of salt and realize that they are just trying to help. Anyone who has not been through this same situation will never fully understand what you are going through, especially caring for an elderly or disabled loved one. It is not the same as raising children. Children will become more self-sufficient as they grow and eventually be able to take care of themselves and move out on their own. Your loved one will most likely decline to one degree or another over time, possibly becoming more and more debilitated and in need of greater care. You may constantly have to modify your routine to accommodate the changing needs of your loved one.

It is a never-ending (except for the inevitable end), ever-evolving process that requires us to constantly adapt our lives, our schedules and our other relationships. Don't ever let anyone belittle you, make you feel like you are doing it wrong, that you are not doing enough, or that it really isn't such a big deal. I have dealt with all of this, from various people, and it can be very upsetting when you are giving it your all every day. Be grateful for those you have in your life who see and acknowledge what you are doing, the hours you put in, the sacrifices you make, the blood, sweat and tears that you shed, and strive to understand what you are going through. They are the ones who matter and deserve to be in your sacred inner circle. Release everyone else and focus on those who really understand, support and appreciate you as you continue doing your amazing, life-giving work.

Practice Extreme Self-Care

One of my favorite resources on the path of personal care is Cheryl Richardson's book, *The Art of Extreme Self-Care*. I highly recommend you get this for yourself and implement the ideas immediately. It is a twelve-part program that offers one strategy a month to transform your life over the course of a year. We all need this constant reminder as we continually get sucked back into our role of caregiving... and giving and giving and giving. We need to have balance, and Cheryl has created a fabulous process you can easily follow to make sure that you are providing yourself with *extreme* self-care. I love the word "extreme" because it seems to imply the level of care that we are giving to others every day, but rarely give to ourselves. We obviously require at least the same (if not more) care for ourselves to maintain the level of giving that we provide. Ideally, we want to take such good care of ourselves that we have an abundance of love and energy that allows our cup to overflow to everyone else.

Do yourself a favor and make this book a part of your daily routine and form the habit of providing extreme care for yourself. It is crucial to your well-being at this time. You need it and deserve it.

Moving onward...

Care for Your Loved One

Create a Balanced Nutrition Plan – For Both of You

Depending on the specific health issues of the person you are caring for, be certain that you have an easy routine in place to make sure their nutritional needs are met and that they are satisfied.

What we eat directly affects not only how we feel physically, but also mentally and emotionally. Certain foods can cloud your thinking and wreak havoc with your feelings. I have a huge sweet tooth and I know that when I give in to a sugar craving, I usually feel pretty awful afterward. I am more emotional and impatient, I don't sleep well, my anxiety level increases and I just have a general feeling of unrest. But when I am eating a more balanced diet that satisfies me, everything runs smoother. I am happier, clearer, sleep more soundly and have more patience and tolerance with everything going on in my life. This applies to you as well as your loved one. There is more to nutrition than just weight maintenance or Type 2 Diabetes management. What you put into your body affects your entire being, which is why I cover all aspects of health in body, mind and spirit.

That said, I do believe in the occasional treat. Food is one of life's greatest pleasures so if you enjoy it responsibly, both you and your loved one can live life to the fullest while still making wise, healthy eating choices.

I have three basic rules I like to share to get people on the road to eating healthier:

1. Avoid high fructose corn syrup. This is a highly processed product, typically made from genetically modified corn, and therefore is not real food. Your body does not recognize it nor does it know how to process it. Ultimately, it gets stored as fat.
2. Avoid hydrogenated oils. This is another type of highly processed item, made by introducing a hydrogen atom to oil to solidify it. It is yet another product that your body does not recognize and will store as fat.
3. Avoid all artificial sweeteners. They are poisonous to your system and can cause

long-term damage to the immune system, the brain and create diseases like Multiple Sclerosis and Lupus. I will go into more detail about this below.

But first, let's focus on the basics: eat real food!

First and foremost – eat lots of fresh vegetables and fruits. Shop on the outside perimeter of the market; that is where you will find the healthiest and most natural foods.

Go organic. This is an important option and absolutely worth the extra cost. The fact that most people do not think twice about paying for cable, satellite or a myriad of other entertainment options each month, but then are hesitant to spend money on nutritious food that will insure their ongoing health and benefit their bodies seems a bit crazy to me. It appears that our priorities are a little (actually a lot) out of whack. Wouldn't you rather pay for better quality food (which is nature's medicine) now than spend even more money on doctor visits, invasive treatments and prescription drugs later? Put your nutritional needs first and balance your budget accordingly. Check out local farmer's markets for fresh, local and reasonably priced organic food. You will also be helping to support your local economy, including small businesses. That's a double win!

These days it's easy to make a quick, tasty, healthy meal with products like the NutriBullet. Just throw in fruits, vegetables and a little water and you have a nutrient-packed drink in minutes with easy clean-up.

Juicing is also a great way to get an abundance of nutrients in one glass. I love putting in mostly greens, with an apple to sweeten it. It's a totally filling, satisfying drink that my body actually craves now. If you have the means to invest in a juicer, it will be worth it. I would recommend the Breville brand – they have several models at all price points so it's easy to find one to fit your needs and budget. (I'm sure you get 20% off coupons to Bed, Bath & Beyond in the mail, so that makes it even more affordable). The juicer takes a bit more work to clean than the NutriBullet and honestly, I would suggest having both appliances if you are able. It's more than worth it to have a few gadgets that make preparing healthy meals and snacks easy, quick and convenient.

Consider going gluten-free, especially if your loved one has Type 2 Diabetes, Dementia or Alzheimer's disease. This means no wheat of any kind. It may sound outrageous to lifelong bread lovers, but believe me, there are plenty of gluten-free products available to satisfy every taste. Studies show a connection between wheat consumption and brain function in Dementia and Alzheimer's, so eliminating grains may improve brain function in addition to increasing overall health.

Going gluten-free will eliminate a lot of sugars and grains that cause inflammation, which is a great preventative measure against autoimmune diseases and issues such as migraines and digestive problems.

My mom has been gluten-free for quite a while, and we were happily surprised when she effortlessly lost almost thirty pounds over a six-month period. She also has heightened clarity and better digestion, mood and memory. Her blood pressure is normal, her cholesterol numbers are great, and her blood sugar levels are often below normal for a person *without* diabetes! This is one powerful step you can take toward the wellness of your loved one.

An important general rule to follow at all times when shopping for food is to <u>always read the labels!</u> Although they are not consistently 100% accurate or truthful, it's all you have to go on when purchasing processed food. When this is your choice, here are a few things that will make it easier for you:

- If the list is a mile long with ingredients you cannot pronounce, don't buy it.
- If it has a short list of recognizable ingredients, it's most likely a good choice.
- Remember that the first ingredient is the most important – that is what primarily makes up the product. The lesser amount of the ingredient, the lower it will be on the list. Watch the sodium

and sugar levels and make sure they are within reasonable levels. Sugar should not be higher than 10g and sodium should stay below 500g per item.

Use Stevia to sweeten drinks and food, but NO Artificial Sweeteners. Splenda, NutraSweet or any similar products are all chemical-laden and poison to the body and brain and actually increase sugar cravings and weight gain. They come in all kinds of disguises so please avoid anything containing sucralose, aspartame, saccharine or any variation thereof. Again, please do your research. This is another topic that you will find covered thoroughly in many articles on www.mercola.com. Dr. Joseph Mercola has actually written a book called *Sweet Deception* about the truth behind the big business and detrimental effects of artificial sweeteners.

When you buy Stevia, please only buy pure brands, not the bigger name brands you see in TV commercials. The latter are manufactured by the big cola companies and are stripped of many of the beneficial elements. I like Better Stevia, Sweet Leaf and Stevia in the Raw – all good brands. You can use Stevia to sweeten almost anything, so be creative!

Allow your loved one to have a treat regularly. Real sugar in limited amounts once in a while is fine. I make gluten-free oatmeal cookies for my mom and she loves them. It's a treat she looks forward to and it works well with her eating plan.

Create meal plans that are easy to maintain with your busy schedule. If you enjoy cooking, perhaps you will want to make every meal from scratch. Or, depending on your schedule, you may want to pre-prepare meals and freeze them. Find things that are easy to arrange that your loved one enjoys. You want to make certain that they are satisfied and happy with their food.

I would suggest avoiding processed food as much as possible, but when you do buy it, as I said before, be diligent about reading labels. I will be honest and admit that very rarely a will give Mom a TV dinner that I feel is a good choice for her. I have found many options with Healthy Choice, Lean Cuisine and Amy's that I am happy with and Mom enjoys. I choose the selections with low sodium and sugar and the freshest, most basic ingredients. Mom likes them and they are smaller portions, which is perfect for her since she doesn't eat as much these days. It also makes feeding her well easier and more convenient for days when I am busy or having someone else caring for her when I am not available. It's okay to do what works best for your schedule, as long as it's the healthiest, best possible option for your loved one.

If you're confused about how to get started creating healthy meals, find a good nutritionist or Registered

Dietitian to consult with who can get you started and support you in this area.

Eat with your loved one – the company is beneficial for both of you. I will often feed Mom her meal and then run back to do more work in my office (she is eating lunch in the living room as I write this paragraph, I'm embarrassed to say). But, I always sit with her at dinner, whether I am eating with her or not. We enjoy our ritual of watching *Family Feud* while she eats, then we clean her up and get her settled on the couch for *Jeopardy* and *Wheel of Fortune* before she goes to bed. We both enjoy this nighttime ritual.

Make sure your loved one is taking a good probiotic like L. acidophilus and eating enough fermented foods. Gut bacteria is a huge part of overall health, affecting not only digestion, but mental health, mood and the entire immune system. Make sure there are plenty of sources of good gut flora-producing elements in the diet. Include yogurt, probiotic drinks like kefir or Yakult and fermented foods like sauerkraut, pickles, relish and vinegar in your meals. Mom has two L. acidophilus pills a day, a Yakult drink and one container of yogurt most days. I also use sweet relish in her tuna salad (which is actually salmon – healthier for her and contains Omega-3 oils, the benefits of which are listed in the next section). The relish is a fermented food that is good for her digestion and is also a tasty addition to her salad.

Include coconut oil in your cooking and daily supplement regimen. This is another great food that is great for everyone, but especially anyone with a decline in brain function. Coconut is one of the best oils to cook with because it has a high heat point and does not go rancid during cooking. It contains Lauric acid, which is antibacterial, antiviral and improves the immune system and brain function. I give Mom a tablespoon every morning and use it for sautéed vegetables and baked goods.

If your loved one is a picky eater or just doesn't eat much, check into supplemental foods to provide the nutrients they need. I have Mom eat Juice Plus gummies every morning. This product has packed the equivalent of a day's worth of fruits and vegetables into either a pill or a tasty gummy chew. So if they don't have the healthiest eating habits, you can still make sure your loved one will be getting their fruits and veggies. Check www.juiceplus.com for a representative near you. If you'd like to contact my rep, Jamie Leff (a good friend and Registered Dietitian and Nutritionist), you can reach her at http://jamieleff.juiceplus.com/. This is an easy and convenient way to make sure your loved one gets all the nutrients they need.

When you make wise, educated and intuitively sound choices about nutrition, you and your loved one will thrive physically, mentally and emotionally.

Research and Utilize
Appropriate Supplements

Everyone's needs are different, but there are a few suggestions that will benefit anyone. I must again suggest that you do your own research, but here are a few basic guidelines to enhance your loved one's health regimen:

- Make sure there is a good multi-vitamin in the mix appropriate for your loved one's individual needs.
- Omega-3 oil is essential for brain and heart function. Krill oil is the best fish oil available. It's good for the environment and doesn't have the same fishy smell and aftertaste of most fish oil pills. It is a bit more expensive, but you already know how I feel about budgeting for better products for your health.

- Coenzyme Q10 supports enhanced brain function and heart health.
- Vitamin D, at least 5,000 IU/day. I know it sounds high, but unless there is sufficient sun exposure every day, this is the level that will ensure optimal Vitamin D levels. This is crucial for a highly functional immune system and for the prevention of many cancers, including colon, breast and ironically, melanoma. Yes, that's right – lack of sunshine is causing skin cancer. Dr. Mercola also has a book addressing this issue titled, *Dark Deception.* As I said, please do your research and learn the up-to-date facts.

Obviously, there are a myriad of supplements you could be giving your loved one, but don't make it too complicated for either one of you. Keep it simple, cover the basics and make the best decisions you can. If you feel overwhelmed by this, you can consult with an alternative health professional who has experience utilizing supplements and herbs and can help guide you to what is best for you and your loved one.

Take Full Responsibility and Create a Mutually Respectful Health Care Team

When you are creating an alternative routine to care for yourself and your loved one, it can be helpful to find healthcare providers both in the regular medical field and in alternative areas like acupuncture, chiropractic and holistic health. Make sure that you communicate all alternative plans to the doctor so that they are aware of your intentions. Be confident about questioning any drugs or therapies prescribed for your loved one and only agree to what you feel is the right treatment. You are ultimately the one responsible for their health and well-being and you make the final decisions.

Your loved one's health is in your hands. Research the food you are feeding them, the pills they are taking and any other information available regarding their specific health needs.

My favorite resource for all health-related topics is obviously Dr. Joseph Mercola's website, www.mercola.com. It contains a wealth of information about every health issue you can imagine, with natural remedies and alternative health information. Another great website for natural remedies is www.earthclinic.com. There is an abundance of information available on the internet so go have fun doing some surfing!

It's important to create a healthy relationship with your loved one's doctors (and your own), and keep the communication going regarding prescription drugs, ongoing therapies, test results and any other health-related issues. I must emphasize how crucial it is that you stay on top of any issues and keep informed about what's going on with your loved one at all times. You want to be able to make educated and intuitively sound decisions. Most people to go the doctor and blindly take whatever pills or advice that are given, but doctors are not the ones ultimately responsible for their patient's health; each individual is responsible for their own health and well-being. Since your loved one is dependent on you, you become the one responsible for making the best possible decisions for them.

Many doctors may not know much about nutrition and natural remedies and may discourage you from going that route. Please do not let this deter or frighten you. Most of the time, they simply do not have the knowledge to make a recommendation or comment on topics outside of their world of allopathic medicine. You might actually enlighten them to some new resources and help them expand their repertoire with the positive path you are choosing for your loved one. Fortunately, my mother has very kind, compassionate and open-minded doctors who are receptive to and supportive of the way I care for her, primarily from a holistic perspective combined with prescribed drugs that have become necessary for her.

Make sure your health team of doctors and alternative health practitioners are aware that they are a part of a team and that all therapies and providers work in harmony with each other.

Fortunately, there is a new breed of enlightened doctors coming to the forefront of the medical industry, led by the aforementioned Dr. Lissa Rankin. I was thrilled when I discovered Dr. Rankin's book, *Mind Over Medicine*, because this is what I have believed to be true for many years. This is how I cured myself of Lupus – the final aspect after applying every natural remedy, holistic practice and alternative therapy for twenty-six years was a change in my perception and mental state. I have always known the intrinsic value of maintaining balanced emotions and having sources of relaxation and joy in your life, so it was incredibly satisfying to have my internal knowing validated by a medical professional who has done years of research about this topic. So much of the medical industry is about finding problems and treating symptoms with often harmful or invasive treatments or drugs. Traditional Western medicine can instill a great deal of fear into people so I am grateful that there is now more information available to help people understand how to take responsibility for and improve their overall well-being. You can use this information for yourself and your loved one.

You are primarily responsible for your own health and well-being, and for that of your loved one. It is crucial that you stay aware and make educated and conscientious decisions for both of you. Remember, doctors are there to provide guidance and advice on health issues. It is totally up to you whether you choose to follow that advice or take a different route. Find health care professionals who fit your needs and those of your loved one and put together a team that you makes you feel heard, supported, understood and genuinely cared for. It is finally time that we take back our power and acknowledge the fact that we create our lives and state of health. Now, thanks to Dr. Rankin, there is a guide to help you determine where you or your loved one may be out of balance and help you make your own diagnosis, create your own personal prescription and put together a team of health care professionals to support you on the journey to a balanced life. I highly encourage you to read this book and learn how to create mind, body and spiritual balance for yourself and your loved one, so you can both enjoy a healthy and happy life. Thank you, Dr. Rankin, for paving the way for us to create health and well-being.

Monitor Prescription Drugs

Do your research and learn about any prescription drugs that your loved one is taking. Drugs are often over-prescribed, especially to the elderly, who usually do not question the necessity or side effects of what they are taking. Be proactive and find out what drugs are for and when possible, find a natural remedy for any imbalances instead.

You have every right to question what is being prescribed, why, the possible side effects and the potential to eventually eliminate them. Keep in mind that over 200,000 people die every year from prescription drugs, taken as prescribed. Very scary. You must take responsibility and know what you are putting in your body and that of your loved one. You can find information online for just about every prescription drug on the market. Google anything you are not sure about and learn about the purpose, side effects and possible conflicts with other drugs or supplements so you can make the most informed decisions for your loved one and yourself.

Also, keep a list of your loved one's prescription drugs, dosage and daily use printed on your refrigerator in case of an emergency so paramedics can easily find it. This is where they request it be posted and where it can be easily seen.

Stay on top of this as prescriptions and dosages change, and always do what you feel is best.

Obtain Power of Attorney

If it is appropriate and agreeable with any other family members or individuals involved, make sure you (and other appropriate family members) have power of attorney over your loved one's affairs, both financial, medical and if necessary, over their property and real estate. Make sure you know what your loved one prefers (if they are able to communicate that – if not, do your best to honor what you feel they would want), and execute matters to the best of your ability. It is a tremendous help to have these legal issues in place so you can continue to do your job in the easiest and most harmonious way possible.

I am not an authority on this topic as we already had a trust attorney in place that my parents had been working with since they first created their trust over twenty years ago. My brother and I are very fortunate to already have a wonderful attorney who is available to help us with Mom's legal matters and estate planning.

As always I'm going to suggest that you do an online search for help with obtaining power of attorney. www.legalzoom.com is always a good resource if you want to "do-it-yourself". Otherwise, check with eldercare or caregiving associations for referrals and find an attorney you feel comfortable with in your area.

It's always a good idea to address this issue while your loved one is in a more cognitive state, before something may debilitate their decision-making functions, like a stroke or advancing Dementia or Alzheimer's. Ask what their wishes are and assure them that you will carry out those wishes to the best of your ability. Try to make them understand that you have their best interest at heart and that you want to be their voice if or when they do not have one. It can be a very scary thing for someone to give up control of their life choices or affairs, but it will serve them in the long run if they trust the people in place to make decisions for them when the time comes.

Budgeting Money

If your loved one is living on a fixed income, or if you are living on their financial resources, make sure to budget the money wisely and be conscientious of expenses. I am not a money expert, but I am very good at handling both my mother's and my own money. I make sure to put a certain amount away in savings every month and watch how much is spent on extras outside of the regular monthly bills. Every situation is different, so find a financial plan that works well for you. If you need help balancing budgets and handling the financial issues of your loved one on top of your own, seek out some help and guidance that relieves some of that pressure.

Make sure you establish a good relationship with any financial advisors, accountants or attorneys who are handling your loved one's money. Make sure you trust them and that they treat with you with respect and honor your authority over your loved one's affairs. Check in on savings and investments often and don't be afraid to ask questions or make changes that you feel are appropriate. If you are not comfortable with anyone handling the financial affairs of your loved one, find someone that you trust to give you advice. This subject can be extremely stressful, so make it easy on yourself and get the appropriate support you need.

Set Up Automatic Payment for Bills

This step eliminates a lot of work on your part, assuming that you are taking care of the finances of your loved one. Years ago I automated all of our monthly utility and service bills to be paid by credit card. Not only do I *not* have to remember to pay multiple bills each month, but we get points on our credit card in the process! The main advantage here is that it's one less thing to think about every month; you can just pay that credit card bill and be done. If direct withdrawal from a bank account is the only option, just make sure that you receive email notifications when withdrawals are made so you can notate them accordingly in your bank records.

We use one credit card for most bills, and the great benefit is that the points that accumulate eventually pay off part of our future bills. It's a win-win! Give it a try and I'm sure you will love how it will make your financial responsibilities much easier.

Keep Them Physically and Socially Active

Make sure your loved one has some regular physical activity – you want them to move their bodies to some degree every day. These days, Mom's physical activity consists primarily of walking from her bedroom to the living room and kitchen every day. Her senior day care suggested that Mom might benefit from physical therapy, so I checked into it and it has made a huge difference in her mobility and strength.

Mom was given a simple exercise routine that we do at least four times a week, and it has greatly improved her strength, stamina, balance and endurance. I also make her stand up and sit down three times before she has breakfast in the morning. She hates it but I can't tell you what a difference this has made in the strength of her legs and her balance.

If you can get your loved one out for a walk every day, that is a wonderful combination of activity and connecting with nature. I used to take Mom out for a walk several times a week until she became too weak to do the walk. These days I take her out in her wheelchair once in a while so she can still enjoy the benefits of being outside and strolling through the neighborhood. Her primary exercise is now her little morning workout and although it may not seem like much, it has brought about a significant improvement in her physical well-being.

Find a form of movement or exercise works best and is most enjoyable for you and your loved one. Any movement will be tremendously beneficial if done on a regular basis.

Regarding the social aspect…

Check into Senior Daycare Programs

If you have a senior daycare facility near you, check it out and see if it is a good fit for your loved one. Some of these facilities accept government assistance, but if that is not available and you can swing the cost, it is absolutely worth it. This is a great way to keep your loved one active, involved, social and interested in life. Mom goes to a wonderful place near our home called One Generation. They specialize in people with Dementia and Alzheimer's, so their program is specifically focused on activities to stimulate their minds. They also provide day care for children, so there is the added benefit of the older folks interacting with the kids. Mom was a nursery school teacher for thirty-three years and loves the little ones, so she gets a dose of feeding babies and playing with three-year-olds while she's there. She even gives tips to the women working there because of her years of teaching experience, so they really appreciate her help.

A senior day care program has the added benefit of not only providing your loved one with some fun, socialization, activity, connection and involvement with others, but it will give you some much-needed time to yourself to do your own thing and be free of the responsibility for a while. That is often the biggest benefit of all!

Make Sure They Stay in Touch with Friends

It's very important that your loved one have regular interaction with their friends and social groups. Staying social is one of the most important factors in remaining healthy and happy as we grow older, so make sure your loved one has plenty of friends and activities to enjoy.

Make certain that they keep in touch with old friends and arrange phone calls and in-person visits as often as possible. I have my mom call her long-time friends who now live too far away to visit, just to stay in touch and catch up. Often neither one of them knows what's going on and it may be a very repetitive conversation, but the point is that they connect with someone familiar that they know and love, and who brings a sense of comfort, familiarity and good memories.

Mom's best friend since kindergarten lives about an hour away, and I try to make sure to take her down there for a lunchtime visit several times a year. Fortunately, one of my closest friends from high school lives in the same area, so I drop Mom off at her friend's house and then go have lunch with my friend. It's a nice opportunity for them to visit on their own and it gives me a little break to catch up with my girlfriend!

It gets a little trickier when people want to call and chat with Mom or come to the house for a visit. I have to monitor phone conversations and home visits because she doesn't always know what's going on and friends and visitors don't always understand that she is not giving them accurate information. She might tell them something like, "I've been alone in the house for days!" when I'm just out at the market or even in the next room. I also do not like people visiting her alone when I am not here, which some of her friends don't understand. They think they are doing me a favor by stopping by, and I appreciate the fact that they want to see Mom and check in on her, but again, they don't fully understand all of the details about home security that come with an unscheduled or unsupervised visit. Mom is not supposed to open the door to anyone, and does not understand how to properly unlock the doors and then lock them again when someone leaves. I have a select group of friends and neighbors that can visit with Mom who understand the routines I have in place; but the majority of the time, I need to be here.

You may also have people who do not fully understand why you are being such a "control freak" (it's okay to admit, as you are not alone) about visiting with your loved one. Don't expect people to understand your situation unless they have lived it, because if they have, they will totally get it and want to do (or not do) whatever is easiest for you as the caregiver.

Do your best to keep your loved one's social life as active and involved as possible, but also do it in a way that allows you to maintain your sanity. It's a fine balance.

Monitor Their Interactions and Set Boundaries or Eliminate Unhealthy Relationships

This applies to both you and your loved one. We may have people come into our lives who cause tremendous emotional strain and can even be abusive to one degree or another. It is imperative to set firm boundaries with these people and either limit contact or stop seeing them altogether.

It is very important that your loved one feel safe around the people with whom they interact. Anyone who does not have their best interest at heart will cause stress that can have a negative effect on them mentally, emotionally and physically. We need to protect our loved ones from negative and unhealthy people and situations.

On the lighter side, there also may be people who know your loved one well and want to help by sharing their ideas, views and opinions with you, regardless of what you have in place as far as a caregiving routine. There may be some useful information shared that you choose to implement, but often others are acting out of fear of the changes they are seeing and worry that not enough is being done. Keeping in mind the good intentions behind their suggestions, no matter how well-meaning anyone is, you must, in a loving way with appreciation for the thought, set firm boundaries and let others know that you are in charge of this situation and are the ultimate decision-maker.

While some people may become *like* family over the years and feel they can take liberties with your loved one, but bottom line is, they *are not* family and appropriate boundaries must be respected. We always want to maintain good relationships with those we love and especially those who love our loved one. It can be a tricky thing to navigate, but if you're prepared, you will handle it with grace, dignity and love.

Mom has a lot of friends, as mentioned above, and it's always wonderful for her to connect with them. There are a few other friends who contact her once in a while with good intentions, but it may not be beneficial for Mom. Mom was always a great listener, a wonderful shoulder to cry on and always sympathized with and wanted to help everyone with their problems. She was often referred to as "Saint Bobby of Encino". Unfortunately, some people still call to vent their problems to her, even though they know her mental capacity has diminished. In addition, they sometimes call me separately to express their distress at how much she has declined mentally and question my methods of caring for her. I understand and appreciate their concern because it comes from a place of love for my mom. However, it can become tiring and frustrating. Don't let others who are not in your shoes or living your experience make you doubt yourself, the care you are providing, or your methods. You are always doing the best you can. It can be upsetting, but just realize that these people are unsettled and confused by their own loss regarding the change in their friend's personality and inability to be there for them.

We have also had the issue of people calling Mom when I am not home. This can be a real problem if it's a sales person, or friends who want to catch up or attempt to make plans for a visit with her without consulting me. I now have Mom's phone calls go directly to voicemail so we can check and respond to messages more easily and avoid any confusion or miscommunication. Anyone that we talk to regularly has my phone number and knows to contact me directly if they want to talk to Mom. I've just had to train a few people.

However you can arrange it, try to make sure all communication goes through you. It can be rather exhausting, but if you can establish a clear routine that everyone understands, it can work out well for everyone in the long run.

Remember that everyone's energy affects you and your loved one. Be selective about who you allow into your space and handle relationships appropriately.

Get a Baby Monitor

This is a very recent addition to our routine. My bedroom is at opposite end of the house from Mom's, so I don't always hear her if she is calling to me during the night. I sleep a lot more lightly these days, always keeping one ear open for her but I still I may not hear her if she's calling me.

The other night she was having trouble getting out of bed to go to the bathroom and I didn't hear her for quite a while. When I finally was awakened and heard her calling, I felt bad that she had been struggling without my help. Because of being jarred out of sleep and after helping her, I was wide awake so I went online and found a great baby monitor on Amazon. com and ordered it for delivery the next day.

I would suggest spending a little more for better quality and features like a clearer connection without interference or picking up the neighbor's conversations. Especially look for a walkie-talkie feature built into the parent unit. The one I ordered for Mom has this and if I hear her calling, I can talk to her from my end and let her know I'm coming. Or, if she wants to get up early from her nap while I'm still trying to get a few minutes of rest, I can let her know it's not time to get up yet without having to get up and walk to the other side of the house to tell her. I love that. Needless to say, as caregivers we don't usually get all the rest we need, so every extra few minutes we have to ourselves matters!

I am also able to leave the parent unit with our neighbor if I'm going out for a few hours so he can hear her and respond if she is confused, needs help with something or assistance to the bathroom. This is one of the best investments I've made toward Mom's care so far and I highly recommend that you look into getting a baby monitor for yourself. It will give you both tremendous peace of mind.

If a Fall Occurs

First, breathe and stay calm. It can be upsetting to both of you if your loved one takes a fall. Treat them with love and patience and do not alarm them by overreacting. Keep them calm and assess the situation. Do there appear to be any severe injuries such as a broken bone? Are there any lacerations that would require more than a Band-Aid? If your loved one is unconscious or severely injured, call 911 immediately. If they have a service such as Life Alert, use their button for immediate assistance. If they do not appear to have any major injuries, then allow your loved one to remain where they are until they're ready to move.

This is where an exercise routine can be extremely beneficial for them physically; they will have the muscle strength to assist you in assisting them to get back on their feet – literally. A bit of first aid knowledge is always helpful, so again I am going to suggest that you do some research and brush up on your skills. Ultimately, you must do what feels right to you, whether you decide to call an ambulance, take them to the emergency room or directly to their doctor.

Since I am a holistic consultant and do regular work with energy healing, I don't run to the doctor for every little thing. I bring out my holistic tool box of resources when an incident happens with my mother. I use an energy healing technique called Quantum Touch, which is just directing healing energy through your hands to an injured or painful area. You can do this simply by using your hands and visualizing white light enveloping the area upon which you are focused. I also use Tapping, also known as Emotional Freedom Technique (EFT), which is a form of psychological acupressure, to relieve pain and quicken healing time. Once in a while my mother will have a minor incident – nothing serious, thank goodness – and I always immediately begin doing energy work on her. I also do tapping on her to expedite the healing process and alleviate any pain. But again, you must do what you feel is right to you in your situation.

If you are interested in learning more about these techniques, you can find information at www.thetappingsolution.com and www.quantumtouch.com. You can also contact a local natural health practitioner who does this kind of work. It's wonderful to have some knowledge yourself so that you can apply it immediately if you have a minor incident so let me share more information about this in the next chapter.

Learn About and Utilize Alternative Therapies

Many of the therapies mentioned above can be self-taught with books, videos, online tutorials and information. Tapping (EFT) is a powerful therapy where you tap firmly on various acupressure points in the upper body while verbally addressing an issue and following it up with an affirmation. This helps release the stress or trauma you may be holding on to by reducing the emotional charge of an issue and allowing your mind and body to relax.

Tapping is often referred to as "psychological acupressure" since is it is an effective combination of the two therapies. Tapping can be used on anything and is incredibly effective for working through emotional trauma, negative emotions, physical pain, addictions, phobias and any other problem that may arise. It's always being tried on something new so use it for whatever issue that you or your loved one may be dealing with. If your loved one is not totally alert or able to do the tapping, you can do it for them, tapping on their pressure points and verbally addressing the issue at hand. It is just as effective and extremely powerful. You can find information and instructions about tapping at www.thetappingsolution.com and www.emofree.com.

I have been doing energy work for almost thirty years so I utilize much of what I have found to be the most powerful and helpful practices. I began doing it intuitively, and then studying different forms of hands-on healing. It was just an instinctual practice for me and I would run energy through my hands to anyone who was having any physical discomfort or pain. I am also formally trained and certified in Quantum Touch, also an applied healing method that channels powerful energy to specific areas of the body. There are also many Reiki masters available that do similar work. For me, energy work is all the same and depends on the practitioner. If you're interested in utilizing these methods, find someone you like, trust and with whom you feel a connection; that will yield the most powerful results for you and your loved one.

I began studying massage shortly after I began doing hands-on healing so I that I could more effectively work with clients. I was also drawn to learn massage to help the many friends and co-workers I had who were always stressed out and physically wound up in knots. This was one of the first steps I took toward a career in helping others relieve their tension and feel better.

You don't need formal training to help your loved one. Just a loving touch, rubbing their back, filing their nails, brushing their hair or massaging their feet are all affectionate acts that feel good and demonstrate caring. Making someone else feel good, loved and relaxed is one of the greatest gifts that you can give to them that will also add to their well-being.

Keep Them Clean and Fresh

It is important to have a regular bathing routine in place that is comfortable, dignified, enjoyable and easy for both of you.

There may be accidents that need to be cleaned up every once in a while, so make sure you have the proper tools in place to make it convenient. Is your loved one wearing what I call "special underwear" (adult diapers)? These can be a God-send. There are brands available that are very comfortable and not bulky or detectable under clothing. Keep baby wipes on hand and use them after bowel movements. It's very important for all of us to use moisture to clean up after pooping. Most people don't think about it, but if you got some on your hands, would you just use a dry towel to clean up? Of course not! You would run to the sink and scrub with a lot of soap and water. Your tush, and that of your loved one, need and deserve the same attention to cleansing.

If there is a regular eating plan in place, then hopefully there is a regular pattern of elimination so that you can anticipate when they will be going, and also arrange outings accordingly. I always carry an extra adult diaper and a supply of wet wipes in my purse just in case.

Their bedding also requires some additional attention to make sure they are contented and clean at night. If possible, be certain they have a mattress that is comfortable and appropriate for their needs. Have a nice selection of soft sheets for the different seasons – cotton for warmer weather, flannel for cooler. Comfortable and convenient sleepwear is important, depending on their individual needs. If your loved one wears adult diapers, you might want to also use rubber pants to insure that the bed stays dry. As for the occasional accident, I also suggest that you get a waterproof mattress pad. These two items have saved me from doing hours of extra laundry.

Now, my mom and I have an unusual bathing routine in place that some people think is weird – I just get in the shower with her and wash her. She's my mom, you know? I'm okay with it and so is she, so that's how we roll. Obviously, not a lot of people are going to be comfortable with bathing their loved one this way. However, there are a lot of tools available to make this process easier for you both. When my father was ailing, my mother bought a waterproof stool and my brother installed handles and a hand-held showerhead in the bathtub of the guest bathroom. My parents' bathroom had a square shower so there wasn't much room to move around, and the modified arrangement worked out very well.

When Mom became less mobile, we actually remodeled part of her master bathroom and installed a new floor-to-ceiling shower with rails for her to grasp and a hand-held showerhead to make cleaning and rinsing easier (and steam for me!).

I know not everyone can have a custom shower built, but there are many other options, such as the walk-in bathtub. On a more cost-effective level, consider doing what we did with my father and installing hand rails in your existing bathtub or shower. They need to be able to hold on to something to stay steady. A hand-held shower extension makes cleaning a lot easier, regardless of whether you are showering or bathing them. A seat made for the bathtub or shower will allow your loved one to relax and be comfortable. Make sure you have a slip-proof mat on the tub or shower floor, preferably something with a little cushion so it is softer for their feet. Keep the bathroom warm enough, but not too warm; high temperatures can raise blood pressure and cause them to get dizzy. Again, comfort, dignity and ease are the goals here.

Use soap with as few chemicals as possible. Most likely, your loved one is already on prescription medications, so you want to limit the chemicals in the other products they are using. Soap with too much fragrance, laureth sulfates, antibacterial chemicals or any other unnecessary ingredients are going to be directly absorbed into the skin, adding to the chemical overload in your loved one's system. Opt for something simple like Ivory, or my favorite, Dr. Bronner's Castile Soap. Get a good exfoliating tool like a loofah or mesh sponge or glove and use it all over their body to eliminate dead skin cells and stimulate circulation. It's important for all of us to exfoliate on a regular basis, and if your loved one is a bit sedentary, the stimulation is especially good for their immune system.

After a shower or bath is a good time to trim toe nails and use a pumice stone or other foot file to eliminate calluses. It's vital that their feet stay healthy to maintain their balance in walking. Foot health is especially important for diabetics. Regularly check their feet and between toes for any cuts or injuries, as the blood flow is not as abundant as it should be and healing can often take longer and infection may set in.

Make sure towels are soft and clean and the bathroom is warm as you dry them off. Now that they are exfoliated, use a good moisturizer (again, avoid anything with too many chemicals that get directly absorbed into the bloodstream through the skin) all over their body, including face and feet. Always dress them in clean clothes after bathing.

Now you both deserve a rest!

Get Out in the Sun!

I know – you're thinking, "Whaaat?" Yes, you read that right: get out in the sun. It is incredibly important for all of us to get our Vitamin D naturally from the sun. Don't worry about sunburn or skin cancer; I am only talking about 10-20 minutes outside at the height of the sun's power, between 10am and 2pm in most areas. This is when the UVB (beneficial) rays are the strongest. You just need some exposure on the arms or legs (or both), and when the skin gets a little pink, you've had enough. Once again, I am going to recommend Dr. Joseph Mercola's book, *Dark Deception,* about the tremendous benefits of natural sunlight and how people are being given inaccurate information about sun exposure.

Vitamin D deficiency is the cause of many major cancers including breast and colon and believe it or not, melanoma. Please get yourself and your loved one outside for a few minutes whenever the sun is out. It also helps naturally raise serotonin levels (the happy chemicals in your brain that make you feel good), so if you are dealing with any depression issues, this will help. Going out for a walk in the sunshine is a great way to get some exercise, some fresh air and your Vitamin D.

The sun is your friend – don't be afraid of it! Treat it with respect and it will return the love with a strong immune system and glowing, vibrant health.

Help Them Stay Self-Sufficient

Depending on your specific situation, this section may not be practical, but if it is, read on.

Although my mother needs assistance in most things on a daily basis, I make sure that she is still able to do certain things on her own to maintain a bit of her independence and strength. For example, I make sure she is able to get out of bed and use the bathroom by herself, which is crucial, in my opinion. Otherwise I would be getting up several times a night to help her. I can hear her on the baby monitor if she needs help, otherwise she is more confident knowing that she is able to do this by herself with the aid of her cane. Sometimes she forgets how to flush the toilet but the fact that she can go and get back in bed on her own is enough.

Mom doesn't like it when I tell her to do certain things for herself, but if we begin coddling our loved one and treating them as if they are incompetent, they will become more helpless and dependent on us in every area of daily life. This is another form of self-care for you because even preventing just a few things from being added to your loved one's ever-increasing list of needs and requirements will be helpful to you. One small step for them, one giant leap for you!

We want to help them maintain a sense of dignity and pride by emphasizing and encouraging what they are still able to do on their own, no matter how small or insignificant, while their ability to care for themselves is diminishing. Make a practice of helping your loved one do what they can for themselves and cheering them on when they are successful. I have a little cheer I do for my mom whenever she does something on her own: "Give me an M! Give me an O! Give me and M! What does that spell?" And she responds, "Mom!" And I say, "Who's that?" And she says, "ME!" I actually found a Mother's Day card that has cute little hamsters that look like the ones I had when I was younger holding pompoms doing this cheer, so I play that for her often as well. It's important to have fun with all of this!

If you are able to begin this practice early on in their experience of needing to be cared for, it will increase their level of independence and keep them from declining as quickly in their condition. Even though they may complain, it will give them a feeling of accomplishment and give you a little bit of relief. Obviously there will be limits to what you can expect of a loved one with their health issues, so use your best judgment and choose wisely where to encourage them in doing for themselves.

Make Them Feel Needed and Wanted

It's important to make your loved one feel that their life still has purpose, otherwise they may get depressed and begin thinking things like, "Why am I here? It's time for me to go". If they feel that they are a burden to you or the family, they may feel guilty and want to die more quickly to take the pressure off of you.

It's not always easy to get them out of this state of mind, but often actions speak louder than words. We can tell someone all day that they are not a burden, but they see the sacrifices that you make, the work you do and how tired you may be. There's not a lot we can do about the basic daily facts of our situation, but we can exert the effort to make our loved one feel loved, wanted and valued.

Make a point of asking their advice about something they are (or were) knowledgeable about. Even if they don't remember or can't give a complete answer, they will feel valuable just because you asked. Ask for personal advice and their opinion on certain matters so that they feel they've made a positive contribution in your life. Ask them about events in history that they personally experienced. Most of our elderly loved ones can remember what happened fifty years ago more accurately than what they had for breakfast that morning. They love to talk about their lives, their memories and their experiences, so ask often and let them tell the same stories over and over. You might even want to record them for posterity. Believe me, you will be glad you asked when they are gone.

I ask my mother for advice whenever I can and I still have her kiss my boo-boos when I hurt myself. There is just something special about a mother's touch. We recently had an earthquake (they terrify me) and Mom asked if I wanted to get into bed with her for a while (I did and we both felt better). I know these little things make her feel good that she is still able to be "Mom" to a certain degree.

If you have a veteran in your care, ask about their military experience and express your appreciation for their service. Veterans have amazing stories to tell and they have lived and created an amazing part of history. Allow them to share their stories so they know their experience has not been forgotten. You will get a private lesson in world history that you will never find in any book.

Make sure you include your loved one in conversations and make them feel involved in what is being discussed, even if they have no clue about what you're talking about. They just want to feel like they're still taking part in their own life experience. Engage them with things that interest them, like their favorite movies, TV shows, magazines or books.

I'm sure you can find many of your own ways to make your loved one feel needed, wanted and valid. Just make the effort with them – that's all that matters.

Have Them Listen to Their Favorite Music

Recent studies have shown the incredibly beneficial effect that music is playing in the lives of Alzheimer's patients. Those who are usually quiet and unresponsive will become extremely animated and excited when they hear their favorite music from their era.

My mom is from the Big Band era, so she loves Glenn Miller, Benny Goodman, The Andrews Sisters, etc. I keep a CD in the car that has music from the World War II era and she sings along and loves hearing all of her favorite tunes from her youth. It's amazing to watch her transform and get so happy just from listening to her music. She also remembers all the lyrics! This is great for people with Dementia and Alzheimer's and it's amazing to watch how music stimulates them.

If you know what your loved one's favorite tunes are, get them something to listen with, whether a CD player or an iPod, load it up with their favorite songs and put it on for them often. You will be amazed at how happy it makes them and how long they will stay blissfully occupied reliving their youth. You may even start hearing more stories about their years in high school and as a young adult.

If you want to see the incredible, beneficial effect of music on the elderly, do a search on www.youtube.com for music and memory, or music and Alzheimer's patients. You will find some beautiful stories there. You can also visit http://musicandmemory.org/,which is the organization that produced many of the videos about this amazing discovery.

We all know that music heals the soul, and here is a very tangible example that can transform lives. Let the music play!

If Possible, Get a Furry Friend

If you don't already have one, a pet can be tremendously beneficial for both you and your loved one. Yes, it adds more responsibility to your plate, but the emotional benefits are worth it. Cats are ideal because of their independent nature. Dogs are wonderful companions too, but require more time, attention and maintenance.

Consider getting a lap cat to keep your loved one company. The shelters are overflowing with animals that need good homes where they will be loved, and there are actually programs in place for the elderly to adopt older cats. These cats are harder to place in homes because of their advanced age, but because they are older, they are usually more mellow and affectionate – a perfect match for an elderly or home-bound person. The cost can be minimal: just food, kitty litter and a few toys. If you keep this new friend as an indoor cat exclusively, there is no need to run to the vet for annual shots. As a holistic consultant, I am in favor of avoiding unnecessary vaccinations, shots, medications or treatment when there really is no need, or when natural remedies will suffice. That will save you some money. This is another area of research if you are interested in taking the natural route with your pet's health.

There are a multitude of health benefits in having a pet, such as lowering blood pressure, improving health and longevity and relieving depression. According to the article,, "Why You May Be Healthier if You Own a Pet..." dated April 7, 2010 from www.mercola.com, a pet can be especially beneficial to seniors, who have been known to have fewer doctor visits, feel safer at home, have fewer minor health and psychological problems and often a decreased need for medication.

Having a pet gives your loved one that sense of purpose that I mentioned earlier, a knowledge that they are helping to take care of and love another living being. These animals are instinctually aware of when they are living with someone with special needs and are usually more attentive and loving. And you can take advantage of having a pet to cuddle with and love since it will also help your health by lowering your blood pressure, providing some affection and allowing you to relax for a moment.

Our older cat, Lovey, is always checking on my Mom, staying close throughout the day, sleeping with her at night and during naps, sitting in her lap, and always appearing to keep a watchful eye. Mom loves her and feels that Lovey is "her" cat. This is pretty amazing for a woman who grew up allergic to anything with fur! It's a bit of a miracle, actually. Because of this allergy, the only pets I had growing up were hamsters and goldfish. Now we have an abundance of kitty love in the house and Mom is reaping the benefits of it in her later years. I hope you are able to provide the same for your loved one.

Aim to Be Patient and Compassionate

Believe me, I know how frustrating this caregiving role can be. Some days it feels like you have no life of your own and you never know when (or if) you will get your life back. You may often lose your patience and snap at your loved one, forgetting that they are doing the best they can in their current state. Sometimes you may feel guilty if you find yourself thinking about when your loved one will pass on. It can wreak havoc on your emotions. I know it was difficult for me to get my business going because so much of my energy was tied up with Mom and my schedule around her. I struggled with this for years, often losing my temper and getting mad at her for being the way she was. I had to regularly step back and realize that this was my Mom, who has done everything for me. I had to remind myself of how much I love her and want her to feel good, safe and loved.

There is a great point I learned in a caregiver support group: what you primarily need to provide for your loved one, other than the basics of food, shelter and clothing, are to make sure they feel safe and loved. Keep this simple message in mind and be easy on yourself when you are feeling tired or impatient. This role takes a lot of compassion, so begin with providing that for yourself first. Acknowledge that you are doing your best, and then have compassion for your loved one in their situation. I'm sure this is not how they imagined their life would be in their later years. Know that you are making a huge difference in their life by creating a wonderful life for them. Remember to be patient with yourself and you will then have more patience with your loved one.

Laugh, Have Fun and Maintain Your Sense of Humor

I joke with Mom about her memory and our living situation all the time. Having fun is incredibly important in this situation; you may get too caught up in your negative emotions otherwise. Find things to laugh about as often as possible. It keeps things light and will improve the overall health and well-being of you and your loved one. Laughing and joking around actually helps Mom remember things more easily. She does better when she's relaxed and not feeling like she is being scrutinized or judged for any decline in her mental abilities. I often see her trying to "perform" around family and friends to appear more together than she actually is. I want her to relax, be comfortable and be herself.

There are a few things that Mom does on a regular basis that get us both laughing. Every morning when I wake her up, I ask her, "How are you feeling?" She always responds, "With my hands." Some mornings, she knows the routine so well that she just looks at me and laughs and wiggles her fingers, knowing that I already know what she's going to say.

She also loves to comment on the commercials that run during her game shows, advertising funeral insurance. Mom took care of her funeral arrangements and paid for them years ago, so she loves to smile at me and declare, "I'm already taken care of and paid for! Isn't that nice?" I always assure her that it *is* very nice and we really appreciate that she already took care of that for us.

Both of these rituals happen every single day. It's great to see that in spite of her mental decline, she always remembers her little comedy routines, and that the wheels are still turning. In fact, she has been pretty stable with very little decline in the past few years, which I credit in part to keeping things lighthearted every day.

Not everyone sees the positive in Mom's behavior on a daily basis because they don't see her as often. Friends and family often get upset because they feel Mom is "gone", but I think we are incredibly fortunate to still have her here physically, and also still be able to enjoy her company in the moment. It's a nice reminder to all of us that that is all we really have anyway – this present moment.

The point is to take advantage of the time you have with your loved one. Make the most of it and keep a light, happy atmosphere. Laugh and have fun as often as possible!

It's Okay to Let Them Sleep

My Mom sleeps quite a bit these days. That's how things have evolved in our schedule and it works out fine for both of us. People tend to sleep more when they get older, so just being conscious about when and where they sleep can be beneficial. Mom goes to bed quite early, and she's tired around 8pm, after *Jeopardy* and *Wheel of Fortune*, of course. If we have no appointments or day care in the morning, I usually let her sleep in a bit. Then she takes a nap after lunch in the afternoon. It's good to have them on a regular schedule if their memory is failing. It gives them a consistent, daily sense of routine that can help them remember what they do and when they do it each day.

I have Mom take her afternoon nap in her bedroom where she is comfortable and close to her bathroom. It's much safer and easier for her, and the rest of the house is quiet so I am able to do my work in peace or have some quiet time to myself. As you know, the elderly often lose some of their hearing, so the TV volume can be quite loud at times. This is another reason that I let her sleep more often. Mom isn't interested in reading or knitting anymore, and it's too much of a hassle and stress to both of us to get her out of the house as often as we used to. On a typical day, Mom spends most of her waking hours in front of the TV with the volume blasting, which is not good for her mind or my peace of mind. In my opinion, sleep is the better alternative. As long as your loved one is still happy and healthy, adjust their sleep schedule to what works for their well-being and your sanity.

Take Them Out for Some Fun!

Find what your loved one enjoys doing and provide that for them as often as possible. It might be something as simple as getting outside for a walk, a short stroll in their wheelchair, visiting with friends, seeing their grandchildren or playing cards. Just sitting outside and enjoying nature can brighten their day.

I like to take my mom to the movies, even if she doesn't know what's going on or can't follow the storyline. She loves going out to lunch, even if she falls asleep at the table, can't remember where we are or why we're there. She just loves the idea of going out to eat, so we do it on occasion. My niece and I like to take Mom to Disneyland once in a while for a fun outing. It's good for all of us.

I am a huge proponent of having fun, no matter what your age. It makes you feel good, raises your serotonin levels ("feel-good" chemicals in your brain) and improves your overall health. Don't you feel great when you're having fun? I will again recommend watching the Twilight Zone episode entitled, "Kick the Can". It beautifully demonstrates my point.

Imagine how wonderful having fun is for your loved one, especially when it may feel like it's not an option for them anymore. Get creative and get out for some fun!

Get Comfortable with Conversations about "Later"

It doesn't serve anyone to avoid discussing the inevitable. Death is not as scary as it seems. It will give everyone peace of mind to know what your loved one wants after they are gone. When you discuss these issues while they are still coherent enough to make conscious decisions, you will feel better when the time comes to expedite their wishes.

During those two years when my father was in and out of the hospital, there were times when he was not able to communicate. We knew he wanted to be cremated but he kept changing his mind about what we should do with the ashes. "I want to be scattered in the ocean." "No, the ocean is too cold… I don't know… " One day when he was in an alert state of consciousness, I told him that he needed to make a decision and tell me what he wanted so we could be sure to carry out his wishes. He finally decided on being split up into thirds – a third of his ashes scattered in the ocean (when the time came we unknowingly attempted this against the wind and much of my father ended up on my white pants), a third scattered over his parents' grave at the veteran's cemetery and a third to be saved and added to my mother's ashes when the time came. Finally – what a relief! We carried this out exactly as he requested when he passed away a couple of years later. The last third of my father is still in my bedroom right now waiting for my mother. Fortunately, Mom always knew she wanted to be laid to rest in the niche at Forest Lawn with her parents and her older sister (Tanna, whom I am named after). Done and done!

I think this topic is so important that I have already informed my nieces about what I want done with my ashes when I am gone, and that a trip to Disneyland and Maui will be in order for them! As I said, fun is essential, even in death.

Some people don't like to talk about this and will avoid it at all costs – my husband included. It took me a few years to drag it out of him, but now I know his wishes and we don't need to discuss it again. We need to know what our loved ones want in the case of their death; you never know what is going to happen or when your time will come. If this occurs before you are ready, with no knowledge or preparation, then you will have to deal with making important decisions in the midst of your grief. This just adds more unnecessary stress to an already devastating time in your life. The discussion about "later" is for the benefit of everyone involved.

It makes me feel better knowing what is wanted so that it can be carried out later with ease. We always hope that we won't have to think about this until far into the future, but either way, it's nice to have decisions made and plans taken care of so you don't have to think about it again until the time comes.

Have a sense of humor about the death discussion, and make your loved one feel comfortable about where they are in their life, whether they have a few months or a good many years left. It's just another part of life and a transition into their next adventure.

Extra Help

If you are getting overwhelmed with the care of your loved one by yourself and are planning on keeping them at home, you may need to seek out additional help. This is nothing to feel bad about. You are only one person and you are human. You don't need to do it all yourself and you don't have to be perfect. It's okay to ask for help. When you are ready for this step, make sure that you have some reputable, reliable resources available to explore. Obtain references from reliable sources and people that you trust. You may have a personal reference for an individual who can provide the care you need, or you may want to check with an organization that specializes in providing caregivers. This kind of support is readily available these days. We see commercials for this kind of thing on TV all the time now, like www.care.com. There are a multitude of other resources available, so do an online search and find what works best for you in your area.

I actually have close friend, Anne, who is an eldercare expert and is our primary private caregiver on the weekends and at other times when I need to be away. I am so grateful for her and her incredible support. Our neighbor, David is another amazing source of help with Mom. He runs over quite a bit for me when I need to be away for a few hours and I am so grateful to have him right next door. Mom loves the male attention and refers to David as her "boyfriend". Fortunately his wife is okay with this.

Check with reliable and trustworthy friends and neighbors to see who is willing and able to help you out once in a while. I wish you the same amazing assistance in your situation that I have in mine.

Hospice Care

My only personal experience with hospice care was when my father was dying, and we were very grateful for the help and expertise during a confusing and sad time.

When your loved one is declining and in need of more care than you can provide, check into hospice care, not only to support them in their transition, but also for you. Everyone's situation is different at this point, so find support that fits your specific needs (and those of your loved one) to make this time easier for both of you.

It can be an exhausting time of waiting and wondering while experiencing a multitude of emotions. I remember my father hanging on much longer than we expected. He didn't eat for three weeks and his body was wasting away and becoming increasingly uncomfortable. I couldn't understand what was taking so long... and although I didn't want to lose my Daddy, I knew it was his time (past it, it seemed), and I didn't want him to suffer any longer. I actually got mad at God for dragging this out for so long. But during that time I took advantage of my father still being here in the physical and sat with him, talked to him, and when he was too out of it on morphine I just held his hand or snuggled next to him. I focused on feeling his spirit rather than witnessing his deteriorating physical state, and I am grateful for every last moment I had with him.

Check with your loved one's insurance plan about obtaining hospice care. If you need to look outside of their plan for help, one of the best resources I have found that provides extensive, thorough and clear information is the International Association for Hospice and Palliative Care. You can check them out at www.hospicecare.com to learn more about the services available to assist and support you at that point in time.

It can be a great comfort to have hospice care to see to the daily details and extraneous tasks and even provide some emotional support so that you can focus on spending quality time with your loved one during their final days.

And Lastly...

Appreciate the great gift in your role as a Caregiver, and honor it for the special opportunity it is to enhance the life of another from the most loving, giving, compassionate part of yourself. The work you are doing right now is priceless, and even though it may feel as though your efforts are often unappreciated and your life is on hold and filled with restrictions. Know that this experience will benefit you in ways you can never imagine. You will look back and treasure the time you had with your loved one, knowing that you made their life better for a while. Do your best, get the support you need, relax about it all, have fun whenever possible and most importantly, ***take care of yourself***. Enjoy this adventure with your loved one and know you are making a difference.

Remember that it is temporary, you are not alone and that all is well.

All my love to you,
Tanna

About The Author

Tanna Marshall is an expert in understanding how to use your energetic vibration to heal your body, attract your perfect partner and embrace the infinite possibilities of your life. She has invested over 25 years researching, studying, and designing programs that give people the tools and inspiration to understand their emotional vibration and use it to pursue their dreams. As a Certified Law of Attraction Life Coach and Certified Holistic Health Practitioner, she works with women to relieve stress, improve health, release limiting patterns and understand the power of their thoughts and emotions to manifest their desires. In her first book, *Living Peacefully in a Big City: A Guide to Maintaining Your Sanity, Health and Happiness*, Tanna offers a collection of helpful advice on how to stay balanced in body, mind and spirit. Tanna is also the creator of *Infinite Woman,* a feminine community dedicated to supporting, encouraging and celebrating women. Tanna can also be seen in her weekly video feature *Feel Good Fridays with Tanna Marshall* on youtube. com. For more information about Tanna's work, please visit her on the web at www.TannaMarshall.com.

Legal Disclaimer

All information published in *The Enlightened Caregiver: A Holistic Care Guide for You and Your Loved One* is provided for general education purposes only and is not intended to be a substitute for professional medical advice, diagnosis, or treatment. Always seek the advice of your physician or other qualified health provider with any questions you may have regarding a medical condition. Never disregard professional medical advice or delay seeking it because of something you have read in this book. All matters regarding your health require supervision by a personal physician or other appropriate health professional familiar with your current health status. Always consult your qualified personal health care provider before making any dietary changes.

Tanna Marshall disclaims any liability or warranties of any kind arising directly or indirectly from use of this book and shall not be held liable or responsible for any misunderstanding or misuse of information contained in *The Enlightened Caregiver* or for any loss, damage, or injury caused or alleged to be caused directly or indirectly by any treatment, action, or application of any natural remedy, alternative therapy, food, food source, or dietary supplement discussed in this book.

Throughout this book are links to external sites. These external sites contain information created and maintained by other individuals and organizations and are provided for the user's convenience. Tanna Marshall does not control nor guarantee the accuracy, relevance, timeliness, or completeness of this information. The use of any information provided in this book is solely at your own risk.

Made in the USA
San Bernardino, CA
19 November 2014